The Organ Music of Richard Purvis VOL. 1

Table of Contents

H. T. FitzSimons Company

According to the wishes of Richard Purvis, partial proceeds of royalties from the present and future volumes of his newly published music will form a scholarship for organists interested in learning and applying the orchestral style of playing as favored by him.

For more information contact *The Friends of Richard Purvis* at Post Office Box 6103, Aloha, Oregon 97007-0103, www.richardpurvis.org.

THE FRIENDS *of* **RICHARD PURVIS**

Foreword

The music of Richard Irven Purvis (1913–1994) holds a very special place in American 20th century history. Richard's style has unique melodic, harmonic and rhythmic qualities. Not one to embrace fads, he was conservative in a very liberal, musical way, using the best of many musical styles. He was a master of composing and arranging concise, definitive, colorful and listenable pieces.

Richard's longtime companion, John Shields, was his stalwart supporter. An accomplished vocalist himself, John assisted in many ways over the years including serving as a chorister, console assistant, and helping Richard build the Grace Cathedral Choir of Men and Boys into a nationally recognized body—eventually developing into the Grace Cathedral School for Boys in 1957. Passing away one year after Richard, it was John's hope to have Richard's music republished including selected previously unpublished works.

Their handpicked custodian for Richard's extensive library of published and unpublished manuscripts--plus carefully marked scores--was Donna Parker. A Los Angeles native, Donna was a Purvis student in the early 1970s and was very close with both "adopted fathers" until their deaths.

In 1991 Donna, along with Tom Hazleton (Richard's student and assistant organist at Grace Cathedral for many years) and Portland organist Jonas Nordwall (a longtime Purvis friend and one of his last students) formed *Trio con Brio*. They asked Richard to compose a work for three organs to be played simultaneously. Following Richard's usual obligatory mutterings, he composed the fascinating four movement *Symphonic Suite for Three Organs*, which they later recorded. Following John's death, they wanted to make John's desire a reality by forming *The Friends of Richard Purvis*.

Former Purvis music publisher Fred Bock was contacted about the idea. Very enthusiastic, Fred traveled to Donna's Portland, Oregon home to inspect the library to begin the process. However, Fred's very untimely death put the project on hold.

A few months later, Allan Petker of Fred Bock Music was put in charge of the project. The resulting collections of Purvis music include four previously published compositions and one previously unpublished work.

According to Richard's directions, proceeds from previously published works benefit the Alexander Memorial Organ at Grace Cathedral, and proceeds from the unpublished pieces form a scholarship fund for young organists through *The Friends of Richard Purvis*.

The Purvis Sound

Most of Richard's organ compositions were musically realized for the sound of the great Aeolian-Skinner Pipe Organ in San Francisco's Grace Cathedral, where he was the Organist and Choirmaster for over 25 years. Regarded as one of the finest combinations of organ and building, this organ's tonal palette was enhanced in the early 1950s under Richard's guidance by his good friend, G. Donald Harrison, Aeolian-Skinner's Tonal Director. Careful refinement has continued throughout the years by the present curator, Edward Millington Stout III, who was also influenced by Richard's definitive desires. In the 1940s George Wright had named the famous San Francisco Fox Theatre's Wurlitzer *Ethyl*. Following suit, Grace Cathedral's organ became affectionately known as *Gussie*. Like George and *Ethyl*, Richard and *Gussie* were American musical institutions. George Wright and Richard were good friends and it was not uncommon for the two musical giants to attend each others concerts.

To authentically interpret the music of Richard Purvis, an organist should imagine playing a romantic organ in a large gothic structure, where time can appear to stand still. Richard would often quote Charles Marie Widor's saying, "To be an organist, one must have a vision of eternity."

This type of space or its vision creates opportunities to focus on intense musical phrasing, articulation, very expressive use of the swell pedals, controlled tempi and most important, the use of unique, colorful sounds that define the Richard Purvis sound.

For example, a Purvis signature solo registration is a 4' Flute combined with a 2-2/3' Nazard with tremulant. This combination creates a haunting, lyrical sound. That sound will not occur if the Nazard has a Principal-like tone quality or if the 4' Flute is too colorful or has too much "chiff" in its character. It must also be in an enclosed division so musical nuance can be subtlety enhanced. The distinctive flute stops used by Purvis are the 8' Lieblich Gedeckt, 4' Lieblich Flute and 2 2/3' Nazard. According to Ed Stout, "the secret for that renowned sound lies in the Choir division's tremulant, which is set in the "natural" mode, thereby reminding the listener of a great singer or instrumental soloist. The deep and fast tremulant slightly overdrives the cut-up of the stopped metal pipes, thereby creating a feathery and colorful sound. Purvis insisted that all of the tremulants in the Grace Cathedral organ were adjusted to be in harmony with other musical disciplines and not like most church organ tremolos, which are most often set in a slow mortiferous mode."

When Richard's publications listed Strings, he always meant String Celestes. Grace's organ has four pairs of String Celestes varying in quality from the thin, quiet Echo Celestes in the Swell Division to broad, soaring Gambas in the Solo Division. Organists must use their creativity to recreate those essential qualities on their instruments when performing Purvis compositions. As ever changing color was important to Richard, all of his directions need to be followed as marked. It is just as important as using the appropriate sounds for other historical musical periods.

Early in his life Richard was greatly influenced by many of the 20th century's greatest musicians, whom he had enjoyed listening to, studying with or talking to. These included German organist Sigfried Karg-Elert, French organists Charles Tournamiere and Marcel Dupré, Belgian organist Charles Courboin, Dutch organist Flor Peeters, and American icon George Gershwin. Richard loved to tell the story about explaining the organ's mutations to Gershwin who was considering composing an organ concerto.

Richard was also greatly influenced by the Wurlitzer Theatre Pipe Organ. As a San Francisco native growing up in the 1920s, he heard the finest theatre organists of his time. A favorite was Iris Vining, who played the Paramount Theatre's 4 manual 33 rank Wurlitzer, his favorite theatre organ. Many of Richard's compositions were dedicated to theatre organ giants and good friends Floyd Wright, George Wright and later Bill Thomson, Tom Hazleton, Donna Parker and Lyn Larsen.

Musical Notes

Tom Hazleton's memories of Richard's comments about many pieces in these collections provide insight into their creation. *Carol Rhapsody* was written for Floyd Wright in the 1940s. He asked Richard to compose a medley of Christmas carols that he could play for his program on radio station KPO. Richard often played this piece on his own theatre organ program, performed under the *nom-de-plume*, Don Irvin. "Don's" program was played on Oakland's Chapel of the Chimes Mortuary Wurlitzer (with English Post Horn). It was often included at Richard's legendary Advent Concerts at Grace Cathedral.

The famous setting of *Greensleeves* was actually composed during WWII as Richard sat under fire in a foxhole. Following the liberation of France, Richard's band was the first U.S. Army Band to play in the victory parade through Paris. He was captured by the Germans during the Battle of the Bulge, given up as Missing in Action, and his obituary printed. However, like another organist/composer Olivier Messiaen, he was actually a prisoner of war. Suffering from hunger, cold, filth, and the endless marching for the POW columns, he was helped to survive a head wound by a Jewish doctor who hid medication in his shoes. A friendly German soldier provided him with paper, which allowed many compositions to be created during his imprisonment.

Donna Parker has made note corrections to the original *Greensleeves* printing and registration modifications that Richard gave her to play on organs "other than Gussie." Purvis students were known not to play his printed music as written, since there were the inevitable typographical errors, which Richard would emphatically correct.

Jonas Nordwall and Tom Hazleton assumed the task of realizing two of Richard's unpublished works for these collections.

The Chorale *"O Sacred Head Now Wounded"* was composed using four staves. Richard routinely would prepare each rough draft using a single staff for each manual, later condensing the manuscript to the standard three stave copy. Tom felt that the range of notes exceeded the practical printing range on three staves, so the original four stave version was retained.

Gwalsmai was dedicated to Harold Eineke, a longtime friend of Richard's and fellow Organist-Choirmaster at Spokane, Washington's Episcopal Cathedral. The persistent rhythmic drive created in the pedals must be present at all dynamic levels to achieve Richard's concept.

Lilliburlero was written for Donna Parker in a collection originally titled "A Cheerful Earfull—Five Vignettes for Residence Organs" (later published as "Gentle Moods").

Richard Purvis did not limit his visions to only traditional organ sound, but always looked at the possibilities to create the best musical results. He taught his students how to make music that was meaningful, full of interest and performed with the highest musical integrity. His music makes a very unique legacy to the organ literature of the 20th century. Please enjoy all of these works.

The Friends of Richard Purvis

THE FRIENDS *of* RICHARD PURVIS

www.richardpurvis.org

Dick composing at his desk at home.

Dick celebrates his 80th birthday
with some of his students.

O SACRED HEAD, NOW WOUNDED

SCHEME I (á la Grace Cathedral)

GENERAL PISTON I

MANUAL I (CHOIR)
Erzahler 8'
Erzahler Celeste 8'
Lieblich Flute 4'
Tremulant

MANUAL II (GREAT)
Solo to Great 8'
(SOLO)
English Horn 8'
Flute 4'
Tremulant

PEDAL
Gemshorn 16'
Lieblich Gedeckt 16'
Still Gedackt 8'

GENERAL PISTON II

MANUAL I (CHOIR)
Viola Pomposa 8'
Viola Celeste 8'
Erzahler 8'
Erzahler Celeste 8'
Swell to Choir 8'
(SWELL)
Gamba 8'
Voix Celeste 8'
Echo Viols II 8'
Flauto Dolce 8'
Flute Celeste 8'
Vox Humana 8'
Tremulant

PEDAL
Violone 16'
Gemshorn 16'
Swell to Pedal 8'
Choir to Pedal 8'

SCHEME II (Classic)

GENERAL PISTON I

MANUAL I (CHOIR OR POSITIV)
Gedakt 8'
Koppelflöte 4'

MANUAL II (GREAT)
Cornet V (Flutes 8', 4', 2-2/3', 2', 1-3/5'
Trem. opt.)

PEDAL
Quintaton 16'
Gedackt 8'

GENERAL PISTON II

MANUAL I (CHOIR OR POSITIV)
Principal 8' or Gemshorn 8'

PEDAL
Bourdon 16'
Choir or Positiv to Pedal 8'

HANS LEO HASSLER
Arr. by RICHARD PURVIS
(ASCAP)
Edited by G. Thomas Hazleton

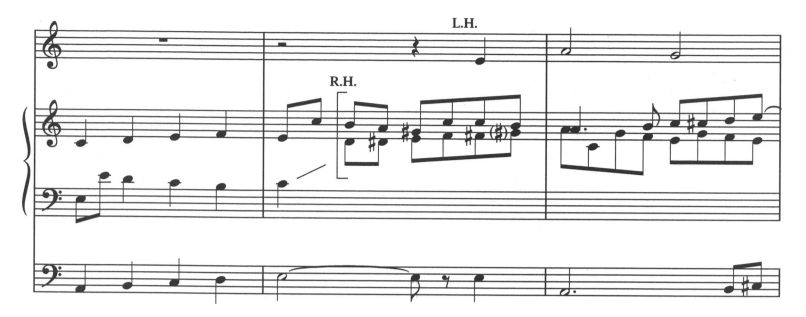

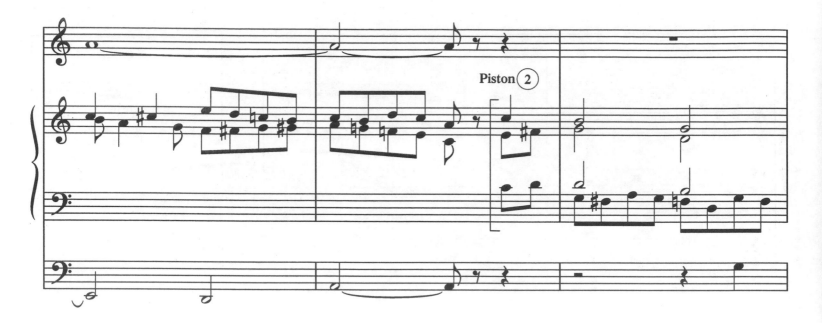

Piston ②

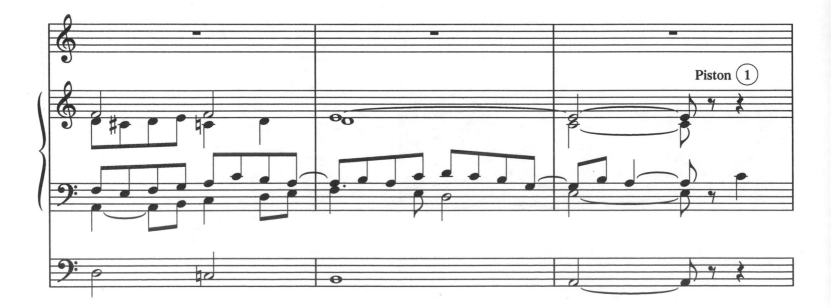

Piston ①

12

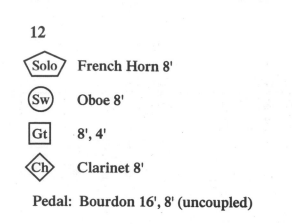

For Dr. C. Harold Einecke

GWALSHMAI*

(From *Four Carol Preludes*)

RICHARD PURVIS
(ASCAP)

Quasi marcia rustico

il pedale non legato

*Gwalshmai is a Welsh Easter carol. It can be found in the Episcopal hymnal.

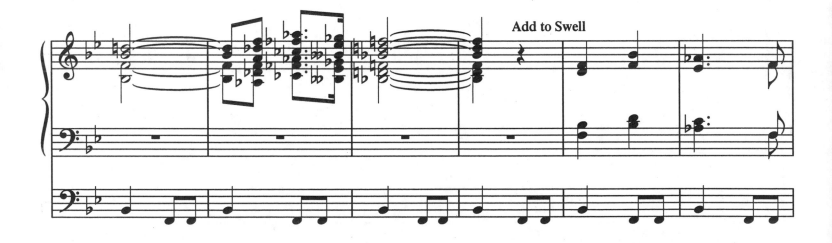

Grandioso

molto allarg. poco a poco

a tempo

Solo to Gt. 16', 8', 4' *fff*

rall. poco a poco al fine

For Claribel G. Thomson

GREENSLEEVES

(From *Four Carol Preludes*)

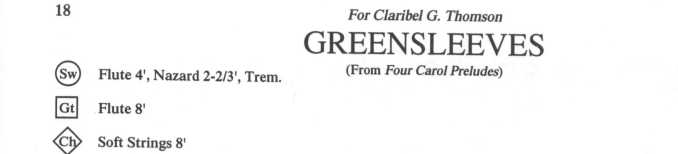

(Sw) Flute 4', Nazard 2-2/3', Trem.

Gt Flute 8'

(Ch) Soft Strings 8'

Pedal: Soft 16', 8' (Choir coupled)

RICHARD PURVIS
(ASCAP)
Edited by Donna Parker

Andante con moto (quasi pastorale)

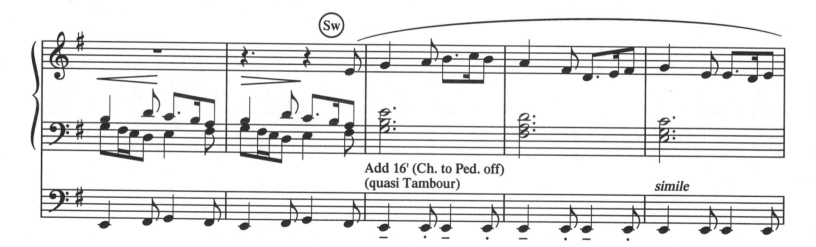

Add 16' (Ch. to Ped. off)
(quasi Tambour)

simile

legato

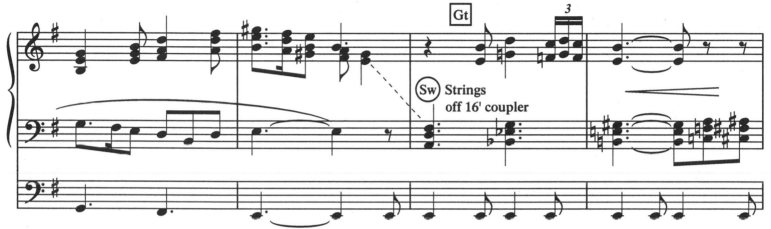

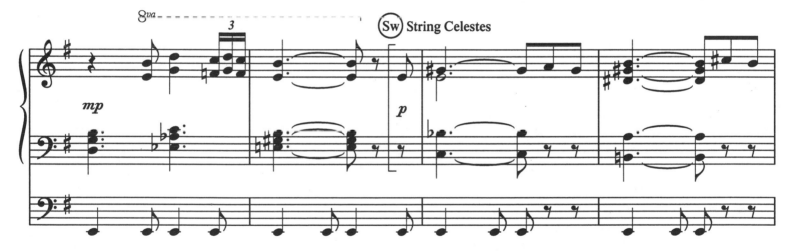

*Played with thumbs

For Floyd Wright

CAROL RHAPSODY

Solo English Horn 8'

Sw Strings, Flutes,
Vox Humana 8' with Tremolo

Gt Chimes

Ch Harp or Celesta (8' and 4')

Pedal Soft 16', 8'

RICHARD PURVIS
(ASCAP)

Lento

Poco piú mosso

Sw: Add 4' coupler

pochissimo rall.

Ch Clarinet 8'

a tempo

Sw

slargando

a tempo

Gt

Solo

Sw

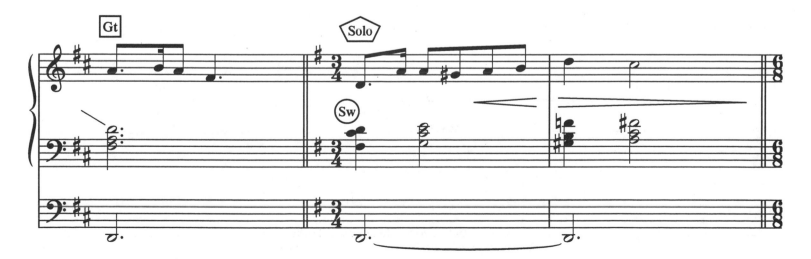

24

Allegro scherzando

Sw. and Gt. Flutes 8', 4', 2'
with light mixtures; Sw. to Gt.

staccato sempre

Increase Pedal

Pedal *mf* 16', 8'
Sw. and Gt. to Ped.

Maestoso

allarg. molto

marcato

Increase Pedal

Open Crescendo Pedal

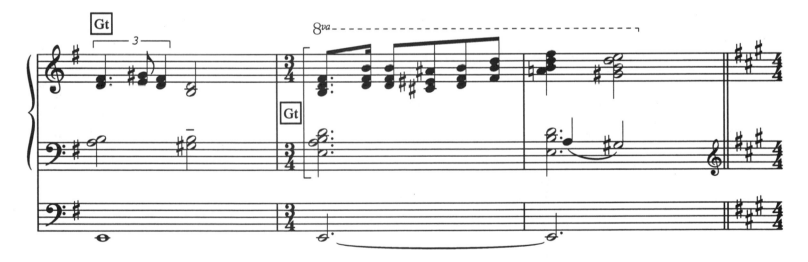

Allegro con fuoco

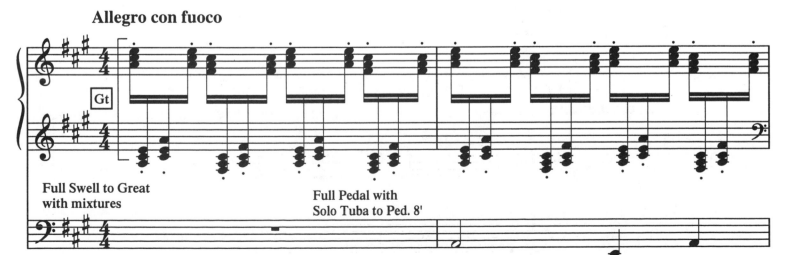

Full Swell to Great
with mixtures

Full Pedal with
Solo Tuba to Ped. 8'

simile

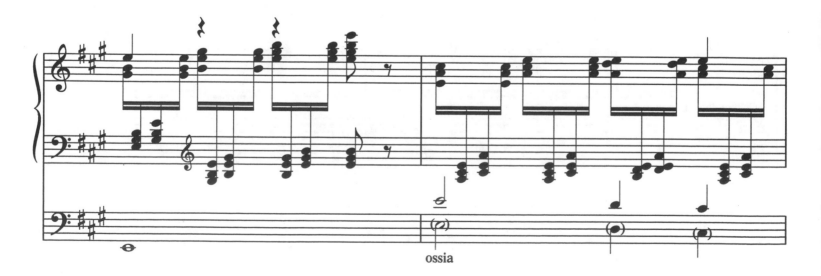

ossia

For Donna Parker

LILLIBURLERO*

CLASSICAL TYPE ORGAN
① Sw. Reed 8′ Flute 4′ Trem.
② Gt. Flutes 8′ & 4′
Pedal 16′ & 8′

THEATRE TYPE ORGAN
① Reed 8′ Tibia 4′ 2⅔′
② Flutes 8′ & 4′
Pedal 16′ & 8′

DRAW BAR ORGAN
① Upper 007 652 000
② Lower 004 300 000
Pedal 4-2

RICHARD PURVIS
(ASCAP)

Andantino (♩ = 112)

*Tune attributed to Henry Purcell.

The Organ Music of Richard Purvis VOL. 2

Including...

Romanza
Communion
Melody in Mauve
An Erin Lilt
Wedding March
(We are proud to include "Wedding March,"
which is published for the first time in volume two.)

THE FRIENDS *of* RICHARD PURVIS

www.richardpurvis.org